The

SEXUALLY

DOMINANT

WOMAN

The

SEXUALLY
DOMINANT
WOMAN

A Workbook for
Nervous Beginners

BY LADY GREEN

greenery press

Cover illustration: W.S. Fisher

Published in the United States by Greenery Press, P.O. Box 5280, Eugene, OR 97405, www.greenerypress.com.

Distributed by SCB Distributors, Gardena, CA.

Contents

1

Could you be a sexually dominant woman?

Yes   No   Maybe

☐   ☐   ☐   I enjoy acting, costume parties and/or role-playing games like "Charades" and "Truth or Dare."

I enjoy costume parties.

☐   ☐   ☐   I am sexually imaginative and enjoy adventures like buying sexy clothes or toys, or having sex in unusual circumstances or environments.

☐ ☐ ☐   I sometimes enjoy sex in which one partner remains passive while the other one "directs the action."

☐ ☐ ☐   I am drawn to "risky" activities like bungee jumping, white-water rafting, mountain climbing and skydiving.

☐ ☐ ☐   I am a good communicator, with the ability to decide what I want and explain it to my partner, as well as to listen carefully to his desires and fantasies.

☐ ☐ ☐   I am "together" enough to take responsibility for my partner's well-being as well as my own during a pre-negotiated time period.

Give yourself 10 points for every "Yes" answer, 5 for every "Maybe," and 0 for every "No." If you score 25 or over, you can probably learn and enjoy the art of sexual domination!

2

How did you get this book?

Perhaps someone important in your life gave you this book. He is probably sitting somewhere as you read this, fervently hoping that you won't be upset or grossed out by what you read here. He gave you the book because he longs to submit to you – maybe by serving you, or receiving strong sensations from you, or being made lovingly helpless by you. I hope that this book will make it possible for the two of you to explore this loving and exciting style of sexuality together.

Or maybe you're submissive yourself, and you've bought this book as a gift for the lady in your life. Good move. I've written it to be as friendly, persuasive and non-threatening as I can; since I wrote the first edition six years ago, it's introduced well over 10,000 men and women to the pleasures of sexual domination. However, your attitude (and hers) will determine whether this book winds up well-thumbed in your nightstand or gathering dust in your garage. Pay special attention to Chapter 12, and good luck.

Or maybe you found this book yourself. You picked it up because you hoped it might hold the key to fantasies you may barely have dared acknowledge even to yourself. If you're like I was, it may take you four or five visits to the bookstore to get up the courage to carry it to the counter and buy it. Don't worry – the person behind the counter has seen people buy much weirder stuff than this; she doesn't care what your fantasies are, she just wants you to buy books.

Whoever you are, and whatever your background, thanks for picking up this book. I hope you get what you want from it.

3

What is sexual domination?

There are probably as many styles of sexual domination as there are sexual dominants. But let's start out by clearing up a couple of misconceptions about this rewarding and popular lovestyle.

"Sadomasochism," a common word used to describe sexual domination and submission (you may also hear it called "S/M" or "BDSM"), is often *mis*used to describe people who are genuinely sick – who use pain or force on those who don't want to participate.

A sexually dominant woman, on the other hand, enjoys giving her lover orders, tying him up and/or giving him strong sensations – but part of her enjoyment comes from the knowledge that her partner is enjoying these things, too.

Sexual domination is a responsible, consensual and non-exploitive way to explore erotic power games.

("Consensual" simply means that you and your partner
have both consented to participate in the scene you do
together.) A good scene is playful (although it may
be very intense), loving, and
intimate, with lots of
communication before, during
and after. These
conditions can only
take place when both
partners are perfectly
clear that they want
to be in the scene
and are
participating of
their own free will.

Part of her enjoyment comes from the knowledge that her partner is enjoying these things, too.

4

Styles of sexual domination

I'm using "sexual domination" as a very loose, general term to describe many different kinds of sexual and non-sexual play. For the purposes of this workbook, I'm going to break it down into three basic categories:

– Playing with helplessness – e.g., bondage and similar activities.

– Playing with roles – exploring "games" such as mistress/slave, governess/child and captor/captive.

– Playing with sensation – giving your partner pain, sexual arousal, sensual stimulation, sensory deprivation and so on.

You'll probably find that most sessions incorporate all three of these kinds of play in varying proportions. Your style will also vary through time, and may change from one partner to the next. Stay flexible and pay a lot of attention to what activities feel comfortable and arousing to you; that's how you'll build your own personal domination "signature."

Many kinds of domination fit only loosely into these categories, and there are many gray areas (such as cross-dressing and fetishes) that, depending on the participants, may or may not include sexual domination. Since this is an introductory workbook, I'm going to dwell on the most common types of domination. Later in this book is an address where you can write to me if you want more information about some of these specialized areas.

An important note: The next several chapters all explain how to do various types of sexual domination activities. Please read them all, and most especially Chapter 10 ("Tips for Physical and Emotional Safety"), before you begin to play.

5

Playing with helplessness

Helplessness play varies in intensity from "pretend bondage" (where you put your partner into a certain position and instruct him to hold that position as though he were tied there) through complicated and ornate bondage that takes years to learn and hours to apply. But most of what you need to know about bondage can be learned quite easily.

For some people, it's important that helplessness be "real" – that no matter how much they struggle, they can't escape. Others wouldn't dream of trying to escape and think padlocks and such are silly. Make sure your expectations and your partner's are in line.

The greatest danger in bondage is compressing the nerves or blood vessels in the bound part. If your partner complains of numbness or tingling, loosen the bondage or unfasten the affected part immediately. Check hands and feet often; if they feel cold to your touch, loosen the bondage.

Never leave your partner alone while he's in bondage! The rule of thumb is to treat someone in bondage as you would a young infant – that is, it's OK to leave the room for a moment to get something or to heighten the suspense, but never go farther than a room or so away, and not for long. If your partner is gagged, it's probably better not to leave at all.

Some people spend a huge amount of time learning and practicing fancy bondage. In reality, though, most people who play with helplessness wind up using only a few basic strategies.

Restraints

(I'm using the word "restraints" to mean any type of bondage that doesn't require that you tie knots.)

–   Arm and leg restraints. Basic leather and nylon cuffs can be bought in many adult boutiques and through mail-order catalogues. These may fasten with Velcro, buckles, or a metal "U" that is threaded through the cuff and locked with a padlock. If you or your submissive prefers "real" bondage, get the locking kind (keep the spare key on your personal key ring so you can't lose it!). For other people, buckles or Velcro are easier.

If you want to play with handcuffs, be sure to get good ones – the cheap ones sold in many adult boutiques are likely to jam, and sometimes don't use a standard handcuff key. Handcuffs should "double lock" – they should have a button to compress that prevents the cuffs from tightening beyond a certain point. Buy a name brand from a store that sells uniforms and supplies for police and security officers; they should cost at least $20. Read the directions carefully. Even good handcuffs, though, can cause problems if applied too tightly or left on for too long. Unless you really like the idea of handcuffs, I recommend that you stick with leather or nylon restraints.

–   Body restraints. The variety of harnesses and other body restraints available through mail-order catalogs is limited only by your budget. Before you invest in expensive body restraints, try a "dry run" using rope; some kinds of commercial restraints are too uncomfortable for a submissive to wear for long.

If you don't have a four-poster bed, one basic body restraint that I do recommend is some sort of "spreader bar" to hold your submissive's legs apart.

A broomstick with eye-bolts screwed into the ends, or a length of PVC pipe with soft rope threaded through it, are inexpensive and work fine.

Another inexpensive and useful body restraint is a "cock ring" – typically a narrow piece of leather about 10" long, with snaps. Fastening it tightly around your partner's cock and balls boosts his sensation there and makes him feel that his genitals are "owned" by you.

– Facial restraints. In many commercial bondage photos, the model is gagged and/or hooded. Many gags and hoods, however, are dangerous. I recommend waiting until you've had some play experience before you try playing with either gags or hoods.

The popular "ball gag" can put a strain on your submissive's jaw, or even make it difficult for him to swallow. It's safer and cheaper to tie a large double or triple knot in the center of a scarf, put the knot in his mouth and tie the scarf behind his head (the fabric absorbs saliva). If you play with gags, you need to agree on a special non-verbal "safe word" (three emphatic, regularly spaced grunts is a good one). Never gag a submissive whose nose is stuffed up!

Hoods which limit your partner's vision and
hearing, but not his breathing or speech, are
basically safe – although it's harder to judge his
reactions when you can't see his face. If you like
the idea of a hood, experiment with a lightweight
pillowcase, or with the spandex models found in
some erotic boutiques.

Blindfolding your submissive is generally safe and
exciting (if you've negotiated it beforehand). The
satin "sleep masks" sold in drugstores make
excellent blindfolds.

–   Knotted bondage. It doesn't take a merit badge to
be a good knotswoman; if your Scouting days are
behind you, just learn how to tie a square knot.
Get someone to show you or buy one of the many
knot books at your bookstore (see the appendix for
suggestions), then practice until you can tie this
knot without thinking about it.

I prefer soft 100% cotton rope for bondage, but it
can be hard to find. The cotton clothesline carried
by some hardware stores is a little stiff and harsh,
but washing it in your washing machine with fabric
softener softens it a bit. Although nylon rope is
very soft and sensuous, knots in it tend to slip.

Silk scarves and neckties are lovely for bondage, but be aware that knots in silk may get very tight. Don't use a scarf unless you're willing to cut it off. (A trip to Goodwill can come in handy here.) Avoid nylon stockings for bondage, since they can chafe and even cut.

Here are a few basic ways to tie up your partner. For purposes of clarity, I'll refer to the bondage material as "rope." A good length for each piece is six to eight feet.

- Hands behind the back. A submissive of average weight and muscularity should be able to have his hands tied behind his back for half an hour or more, but some can't tolerate it at all. Check his hands often for numbness, tingling or coldness. If he's on his back, he'll need one or more pillows under his butt to keep pressure off his wrists.

  Have your partner hold his wrists behind his back, one above the other. Fold the rope in half and place the midpoint against his back and above his arms, with the ends falling down between his arms and his body. Bring the ends up around his wrists and thread them through the midpoint loop. Wrap the folded rope loosely several times around both wrists,

Fold the rope in half and bring the ends
up, threading them through the fold.

Wrap the rope loosely around both
wrists, leaving ends of about one foot.

Wrap the ends in opposite directions
to form a circle called a cinch.

Tighten until firm and tie off in a
square knot.

leaving ends of about one foot. Separate the
ends, then wrap them in opposite directions,
between the wrists and around the loops of
rope, to make a circle called a "cinch." Tighten
the cinch until the wrists are fastened together
firmly but not tightly (you should be able to
insert two fingers between the bondage and
the wrists). Tie in a square knot.

- Hands in front. Have your partner cross his wrists in front of him. Use the same basic tie as "hands behind the back," with the initial loops passing around the place where the wrists cross, and the cinch passing between the wrists.

- Ankles together. You can tie your partner with his legs together, or with his legs crossed at the ankles and spread at the knees. Use the same basic techniques as "hands in back" or "hands in front" above. You may wish to tie the ankles to "hands in back" (a "hog tie"), either face-down or face-up, but be aware that this may be an uncomfortable position that your submissive might not be able to tolerate for long.

- Arms to thighs. An excellent bondage position that most submissives find comfortable for longer periods of time. Have him hold his arms down to his sides with his inner wrists touching the outside of his thighs. Run the rope a couple of times around the wrist and the thigh together, then finish with a cinch between wrist and thigh.

- Spreadeagled. For some submissives, being tied to something is especially scary, so negotiate this before you do it. You can tie him face-up or face-down (if face-down, a pillow under his chest will relieve pressure on his neck). You'll need four pieces of rope. Starting from the midpoint of the rope, wrap it several times around the wrist or ankle, then tie it off with a square knot. Fasten the ends around the bedpost with a bow or square knot. (If the rope chafes or tightens to the point that it's uncomfortable for him, take it off, wrap a washcloth around the limb, and re-tie the rope over the washcloth.)

Here are some types of bondage to be used very carefully, if at all:

- Around the front of the neck. Very, very dangerous. If it's important to you to fasten your partner's hands to his neck, you can buy "slave shackles" with collars that are broad enough to reduce the danger of strangulation. Otherwise, forget it.

- Hands overhead. There are three dangers here. One is that having his hands over his head may make your partner dizzy or faint.

Another danger is that if your partner does faint, you have the problem of how to release him and lower him safely to the floor. You can buy a device called a "panic snap" in mountaineering and horseback riding stores; it's designed to release with a single tug on a strategic point, even under pressure. Better yet, a small block and tackle, rated for twice your partner's weight, will enable you to lower him slowly to the floor. If you like having your partner's hands overhead, invest in one or both of these.

The third danger is that whatever you have him fastened to may break or pull out. If you're not utterly confident of your ability to center an eye-bolt into a ceiling joist or wall stud, hire a carpenter (you can always tell her it's for hanging plants). Test the eye-bolt first by having someone heavy hang from it.

– Suspension. Same problems as "hands overhead," only more so. If you're determined to try it, how about tying him into one of the "hammock chairs" you can buy in import stores?

In general, remember that the atmosphere you've established is often more important to your partner's reaction than the actual bondage you've put him in. You'd be amazed how helpless a submissive can feel with his hands tied behind his back, his eyes blindfolded, and a powerful woman taking control of him! Start slowly, negotiate thoroughly, experiment cautiously – and have fun.

6

Playing with roles

A few dominant women and their submissive partners never play with roles at all – they're simply themselves, whether they're playing or not. Most of us, however, consciously or unconsciously adopt some sort of role during play. We may keep the role inside our heads, or we may act it out with our partner. Acting it out with your partner requires some special skills and knowledge.

It's not necessary that your role fantasies and your partner's coincide for every play session. If he wants to be a naughty little boy getting spanked by his babysitter, and you'd rather be an Amazon priestess testing her slaves with ordeals, you may need to take turns in acting out each other's fantasies. Lots of give-and-take and good communication will help.

Keep in mind that all these roles are for play – just like the "pretend" games you played as a child. If you or your

partner starts to feel really angry or displeased, your
session is almost certain to end badly. Solve the problem as
loving, equal partners – then play after you've cooled down.

Certain roles have been popular with dominant women
and their partners for centuries. Although you may think
of variations on them – and probably think up whole new
ones on your own – here are some ideas about how to work
within basic roles.

–   Mistress and slave. The classic. You own him.
His only purpose is to serve your pleasure. If he
fails, you can punish him; if he succeeds, you
might reward him if you're feeling generous – or
you might punish him anyway, just because you
feel like it.

The basic symbol of slavery is, of course, the
collar. If the two of you have a long-term
committed relationship, it's a wonderful gesture to
have a custom collar made just for him; otherwise,
a basic dog collar (20" is about right for most men)
works fine. He should be kneeling on the floor
when you collar him. Hold the collar to his lips to
be kissed, then look deeply
into his eyes as you fasten
it around his neck. You
might wish to have the
same ceremony as you

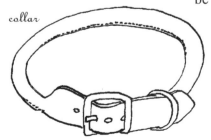

collar

fasten a cock ring around his cock and balls. Instruct him that until you remove the collar, he is to address you as "Mistress."

OK, you've got yourself a collared slave. What now? This is a moment of mild panic for most beginning dominants. Your basic guideline is that activities from here on should be exciting for both of you, but you especially. A few men find it very erotic to be given menial work to do, such as floor-scrubbing; others like to be made to serve a woman's personal needs, such as painting her toenails; still others like to serve her sexually. You need to have a clear idea of what will work for your partner before you begin the session. As the two of you do more mistress-and-slave sessions, you can begin gently expanding his erotic responses.

What if he serves you inadequately? I'll talk more about pain-type "punishments" in the section on "Playing With Sensation." If you or your partner doesn't want to play with pain, simply withholding sexual release is a powerful punishment – make sure he's sexually aroused, but don't let him come until he's pleased you. (By the way, he's a slave – he's not allowed to come without your permission!) Or give him a really obnoxious job to do (here's your chance to get the toilet scrubbed out at last).

If you're happy with his performance, you can reward him with an orgasm. If the two of you don't want to play sexually, find another reward – sometimes just a hug or an approving caress is enough. Come on, you know what kind of things he likes.

Remove his collar with the same ceremony in reverse. Once it's off, you're both out of role. Cuddle, talk, doze together.

–   "Teacher" and child. Many submissives want to revert to a childlike state during play. If your partner wants to become a little boy, you could be his teacher, his babysitter, his nanny, his governess, or even his mommy (careful with this one – you don't want him confusing you with his real mother!).

For most submissives who play in this way, the kick comes from being "naughty." You'll probably need to make up something he's done to be punished for, since it's

Many submissives want to revert to a childlike state during play.

usually not a good idea to bring real-world arguments into dominant play.

Your role lies somewhere between mommy and dominant. The play you do in these roles would be extremely inappropriate for a real child, but can be very erotic for adults!

Say, for example, your "little boy" has been caught stealing candy from the corner store. Start by making him stand in the middle of the room, with his hands folded in front of him and his head down. Scold him harshly for his misdeeds. (Use a childlike name for him – if he's "Robert" in real life, call him "Bobby.") You might wish to make him take off his clothes and stand in the corner while you decide what his punishment will be.

When he's been standing in the corner long enough, take him across your lap or bend him over the back of a chair and spank him. (More about this under "Playing With Sensation.") Depending on his tolerance, this might range from a few symbolic pats to a painful whipping. At the end of it, though, he should feel thoroughly chastened and apologetic; he may even cry. This is your cue to take him into your arms and comfort him. Reward him for his apology appropriately – with sexual play if that's what you've negotiated, or with hugs, caresses, an ice-cream cone or whatever seems appropriate.

–   Captor and captive. These roles work well for submissives who are ambivalent about their submission, since a captive can be a strong and capable individual who's simply been overpowered by force. Variations include Amazon warrior and enemy soldier, rich lady and burglar, Indian maiden and cowboy, and so on.

You might or might not want to include the actual capture in your scene (a toy gun or knife can come in handy). You can also pretend that a small noisemaking device like a whistle causes your captive "intolerable pain."

Bondage, of course, is a must for captivity scenes. Handcuffs fit in well here. (See the cautions on handcuffs in the previous chapter.)

Once you have your captive, you can interrogate him for information. You can put him through an ordeal to prove his bravery. Or you can simply "torture" him for your own pleasure. Any of these can work well in this situation, depending on the specific roles you've chosen. It's smart to know in advance how you're going to end the scene smoothly – if you've agreed to play sexually, perhaps you can reward him for his cooperation; otherwise, you might want to devise a pleasurable ritual to show that he's joined the tribe or whatever.

— Feminization. This is a crucial fantasy for many submissive men; for others it doesn't work at all, so negotiate carefully.

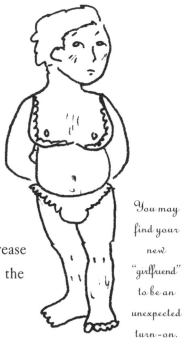

The kick here for the submissive is to be "forced" to dress as a woman. Being feminized is both a humiliation and a pleasure. Usually, you combine the feminization with verbal teasing to increase the humiliation and, thus, the pleasure. (Take it easy with this kind of teasing until you're sure he's OK with it.)

You may find your new "girlfriend" to be an unexpected turn-on.

This is a good fantasy in which to act out your female-supremacist urges. He's a macho pig who needs to learn what it feels like to be a woman. Make him take off his clothes. Tease him (gently or harshly, depending on what you've negotiated) about the cock and balls that make him think he's something special. Make him put on a pair of frilly panties (yours, if they fit him; otherwise you might have to make a preparatory visit to the larger woman's lingerie department). Ask him how he likes the sensuous feeling of women's clothes. If he says he hates it, tell him he needs to experience it further; if he says he likes it, tell him he's going to learn more about it soon.

You get the idea. Slowly but surely, turn him into a "woman." You can even make up his face if you like (and if you've negotiated it). The key turn-ons for him are your scorn for his maleness and the soft, feminine feeling of his womanly clothes. You may find your new "girlfriend" to be an unexpected turn-on for you, too.

Finish the session by rewarding him. For many men who are into feminization, admiring him in his beautiful new "self" is reward enough. If you want to reward him sexually, show him how sexy it feels to receive an orgasm as a woman.

These are four of the most common fantasy scenes – but the number of scenes you can do is limited only by your imagination. As you grow better at role-playing, you may even grow so flexible and intuitive that a session which starts out with a "capturing the burglar" fantasy may turn into a feminization scene... or whatever. As in all aspects of being a dominant woman, communication – before, during and after – is the key to making your scene work.

7

Playing with sensation

One of the most common concerns I hear from women exploring domination is, "But I care about him! How can I *hurt* him?!" That question comes up because we've learned to think of some sensations, like a gentle caress, as "good," and other sensations, like a slap, as "bad" or "painful."

The sexually dominant woman learns to think of sensation simply as a spectrum ranging from gentle to strong. *No sensation is inherently good or bad.* The sensation that would be agony to one submissive is barely a touch to another (or even to the same one at a different time!). As a dominant, you can help your partner explore stronger and stronger sensations.

Thus, instead of dividing this section up into "pain," "arousal" and so on, I'm simply going to discuss how you can give each part of the body a variety of sensations, from gentle to strong. Starting from the top:

Aim the instrument so that the tip will fall on the area where you want him to feel the blow. If you aim too far away, the tip will "wrap" around his body and catch him along the bony side of his ribcage, thereby causing him a great deal more pain than you intended. (Conscientious dominants practice on a pillow or cushion until they can strike exactly where they aim.)

A few safety concerns. Never, ever hit his spine or neck with a strong blow – that's not erotic and it's very dangerous. If you're not sure of your control of the instrument you're using, use your free hand to protect his neck as you strike. Also, striking below the middle of his back (where his ribs end) can damage his kidneys.

– Genitals. It's almost impossible to overstate how protective men are of their cocks and, especially, their balls. (Imagine what it must feel like to wear your internal organs on the outside of your body!) If he lets you give him strong sensations here, that's an honor you should appreciate.

A cock ring will greatly enhance his sensations. If you don't have one, you can wrap a length of soft leather thong or nylon cord several times firmly around the base of his cock and balls and tie it with a square knot.

Many of the techniques you use to give sensation to other parts of the body can also work well on genitals. Clamps can be applied to the loose skin of the scrotum, to the penis, or to the perineum (the little ridge of skin that runs from the back of his balls to his anus). He might even enjoy being lightly whipped on his cock.

A skilled dominant woman can turn an old-fashioned "hand job" into a work of art. The basic, well-lubricated, up-and-down sliding motion you've used a million times is the foundation. But if you give him a few up-and-down slides, then stop to give him a stronger sensation – say, running the tips of your fingernails firmly up his cock, from base to tip – then return to the up-and-down, you can drive him absolutely nuts. Experiment with slapping his cock, pinching, squeezing, even biting (if you've been using a lubricant that doesn't taste too bad)... then return to the up-and-down stimulation. If you have him firmly tied down, you can string him along for an hour or more, until he's going half-insane with frustration. Great fun! (Caution: men can eventually short-circuit and lose their erection if you push this kind of teasing too far. When you sense that he's had about all he can take, be merciful and switch to the straight up-

and-down until he comes – or untie his hand and let him finish himself off.)

A good way to have intercourse with your submissive, if you want, is to tie him face-up and ride him. As he looks up at you, you look tremendously tall and powerful. And you can have fun playing with his nipples and thighs as you take your pleasure.

–   Buttocks and thighs. Most dominant women love butts – I certainly do! They're pretty, they're relatively safe to play with, and they're almost always erotically responsive.

Think of each butt-cheek as a circle divided into fourths. The most erotic part of the butt is the lower, inner fourth (dominants call it the "sweet spot"). You can do lots of wonderful things to his whole butt, but especially here – you can spank it with your hand or with an instrument, put clamps on it, pinch it, pull on the hairs, and a whole lot of other nasty things that you'll undoubtedly think of as you experiment.

Remember what I said earlier about how sensation given over muscle feels best? This creates an interesting phenomenon in buttocks: The more tightly they're stretched over the underlying bone,

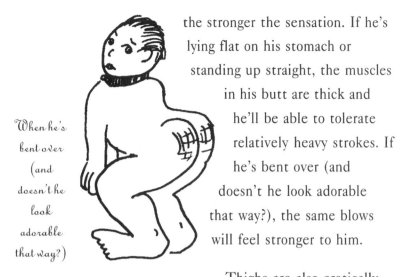

the stronger the sensation. If he's lying flat on his stomach or standing up straight, the muscles in his butt are thick and he'll be able to tolerate relatively heavy strokes. If he's bent over (and doesn't he look adorable that way?), the same blows will feel stronger to him.

When he's bent over (and doesn't he look adorable that way?)

Thighs are also erotically responsive, but they're more sensitive than butts. Be aware that a blow which feels light on the butt will feel stronger on the thighs, especially the inner thighs. Don't hit below mid-thigh; there isn't enough muscle there to protect the delicate tendons and blood vessels at the back of the leg.

Be careful when you're hitting his butt or thighs that his balls are out of harm's way – a blow that feels delicious on his bottom is agony if you strike his testicles by mistake. Use your free hand to protect his balls, have him hold them out of the way himself, or tell him to keep his thighs together. (Experienced male submissives often wear a leather G-string to protect their balls.)

8

Winding down

A good session is a tremendously intimate experience. A sudden or unexpected ending can undermine the wonderful, supportive, intense energy you've worked so hard to build. Therefore, learning to end a session gracefully and lovingly is essential.

It can sometimes be tricky to figure out when a session is over. If you and your partner have agreed to play sexually, the session often ends when you've had as many orgasms as you want and he's had one. Keep in mind that someone who's sexually aroused has a much higher tolerance for pain than he does at other times, so it's a very good idea to stop applying pain *before* he has his orgasm.

If you're not playing sexually, a good way to finish is by giving your partner a goal you want him to meet – "I want you to accept ten more strokes with this paddle before we end this session." That way he can start preparing himself emotionally for the session to end.

When the session is over, untie him as quickly and smoothly as possible. If he's wearing a collar, remove it with the same ceremony you used to put it on. Give him a long, loving hug. Cuddle and snuggle together for a while.

Your partner may be in a very vulnerable, needy state of mind (experienced submissives call it "going under"), and will need lots of protection and affection as he comes down to earth. He may seem giggly or spacey, as though he's been smoking dope; that's the body's natural chemical reaction to strong sensation – the same endorphins that create a "runner's high."

You may also be feeling a little bit spaced out. Endorphins are contagious, and you've been working hard. Please don't try to do any task that takes focus or concentration, especially a dangerous task like driving, until you're feeling one hundred percent yourself again. Don't let him get behind the wheel either – both of you should just take some time to enjoy the aftermath of your session together.

The two of you may feel very hungry or thirsty after the session, so it's a good idea to have food and drinks in the house. When you've both had a chance to come back down to earth, talk about your session – what worked, what didn't, what might be good to try next time.

The next day, talk to him see how he's doing. Once in a while, feelings of sadness, anger or depression may arise for one or both of you after the session. Or he may find physical marks that he hadn't counted on. Even if things went perfectly, it's a good idea to touch bases just to maintain the loving connection you initiated.

9

How will you feel afterwards?

It's not unusual for one or both partners to experience some "aftershocks" after a sexual domination scene – either immediately afterwards, or a day or two later.

You may feel fatigued, depressed, shaky, or even weepy. Your partner may experience some feelings of anger or sadness.

Please, if either of you has these feelings, don't think it's because you've necessarily done anything wrong. Sexual domination is an act of trust and intimacy that brings out deep emotions in many people; that's part of the reason we do it. Think of these feelings as a natural cycle – you were having a wonderful time, you were in a sort of alternate universe, and now you're coming back into the same old world again.

Most of us were brought up to believe that the kinds of things we do in a sexual domination scene are wrong or sinful. Even if we know that our scene was completely consensual and very much desired by everybody involved, it can be hard not to feel guilty at some level.

Also, sexual domination is hard work and a lot of responsibility. Many a woman has gotten confused when she felt exhausted or let down after a scene – after all, wasn't she being a selfish bitch who was getting exactly what she wanted? Well, yes, sort of – but she was also the author, director, stage manager, costumer and lead actor in a whole theatrical production, and that's *tiring*.

The answer to all these issues is to take care of each other. Submissives need to be reassured that they're strong and capable, and that we don't think any less of them now that we've seen their submissive side. Dominants need to be reassured that they're good people and that they did a great job. Be good to each other and the feelings should pass soon.

Once in a long while, a memory or emotion which is painful or troubling may emerge during a scene. Sadly, many of us were abused as children or adults, and almost all of us have had feelings of sadness or anger in our lives which can be accidentally triggered by something we do during sexual domination play. If this happens to you or your partner, and if the feelings don't pass in a week or two, you may want to consider getting some outside help from a therapist or counselor. Resources for finding someone who can help are listed in the appendix.

10

Tips for physical and emotional safety

Before I start you off on your first session, I want to spend a moment making sure you know how to do sexual domination safely. These guidelines have been developed over many years, and are designed to help ensure that you and your partner will be physically and emotionally safe during your play together.

– Safewords. Many submissives enjoy begging for mercy, and it can be difficult to tell when "stop" really means STOP. Before you begin play, you and your partner must agree on a "code" word or words that mean "No kidding, this really isn't working, let's talk." There are three basic criteria for a safeword – it shouldn't be a word that he might want to use during normal play; it shouldn't sound like anything else; and it should be easy for both of you to remember even if you're under stress. Many partners use "yellow" to mean "stop for a minute, something isn't right," and "red" to mean "stop the scene and turn me loose right now." Other commonly used safe words include "safeword" and "mercy."

–   Intoxicants. Use of alcohol, marijuana and other drugs during dominant play can be very dangerous. If you're  stoned, you can get so involved in your own feelings that you lose track of what's happening with your partner; if he is, he can overlook signals from his body that are important for you to know about. If you're a moderate drinker, a single drink before the session is probably OK; more is absolutely not. If you can do without a drink (or a toke, or whatever), err on the side of caution.

–   Negotiation. Well before you begin your scene, you and your partner need to have a long, serious talk about each of your expectations and needs. This is the time to use all the communication skill you've got – because this talk is the single most important predictor of how well your scene will turn out! Here are some questions you'll want to ask your partner, some questions to ask yourself, and some questions to discuss.

For your partner to answer:

- What is your primary turn-on – bondage, pain, role-playing, fetishes?

- Is there anything that you really dislike or are afraid of?

- Do you have any physical limitations – heart trouble, a bad back or knees, hemorrhoids, breathing problems?

- Do you have any emotional "glitches"? Have you been physically or emotionally abused – and, if so, what kinds of stimulation might trigger memories of that abuse? Do you have any phobias?

For you to answer:

- What do you intend to have your partner do? Are you sure that your partner feels OK about doing those things?

- Do you feel safe with your partner? If not, what needs to happen to make you feel safe?

- Are you prepared to handle it if your partner becomes physically ill or emotionally upset?

For both of you to answer and discuss:

– Do you expect to become sexually aroused, or to have an orgasm, during this session? If so, what are your safer-sex standards?

– Safety. Sexual domination is probably no riskier than, say, a long car trip. But, just as you'd be prepared for emergencies on a long car trip, you should be ready for most of the things that could go wrong during your session. Here's a list of the basic supplies and skills you should have:

– A quick release mechanism. You should have some way of turning your partner loose immediately if there's an emergency. Experienced dominants keep a pair of heavy-duty "paramedic's shears," designed to cut through fabric, leather, rope or almost anything else, at arm's reach. If you're just starting out, a good pair of sewing shears is probably OK, but get the paramedic's shears soon (they're about $5 to $10 at medical supply stores). If you play with locking toys like handcuffs, keep the spare key on your own personal key ring so there's no way to lose it. Do a couple of test runs with your scissors and keys to make sure they will work well in an emergency.

– Emergency supplies for your
bedroom or playroom. Keep a
flashlight in a night stand
or other easy-to-find place.
A "blackout light" plugs
into any outlet and turns on
automatically if there's a power
outage. If you don't already have
a small fire extinguisher, get

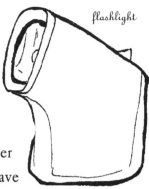

flashlight

one. Your basic first-aid kit should include a plain
bar or pump bottle of unscented or antibacterial
soap, an antibiotic ointment, band-aids, gauze and
adhesive tape. If you or your submissive carries
emergency medication (asthma inhalers,
nitroglycerin tablets and such), both of you should
know where they are and how to administer them.

– A First Aid and CPR (cardiopulmonary
resuscitation) card. Red Cross and other
community groups offer first aid/CPR classes at
minimum cost. If you play with men of middle age
and up, knowing how to perform CPR is essential –
and even if you play with younger or female
partners, it's extremely important. You should be
recertified yearly.

11

A basic session

I remember my first dominant session as though it were yesterday. I had the partner, I had the toys, I had a head full of fantasies... and I had no idea what to do next or how to do it.

Here, therefore, is a step-by-step guide to doing a basic session. You can follow it exactly, or vary it according to your own fantasies and your partner's. I don't recommend that you use this exact session for more than your first dominant experience or two – it's intended as nothing more than "training wheels" to help you build confidence in your own skills and instincts.

In designing this session, I've made the following assumptions:

1.   That you're a woman and your partner is a man.
       (Most of the activities I've suggested, however,

can be easily adapted to playing with a female submissive.)

2.   That you and your partner know each other well enough to feel basically safe with one another.

3.   That you've taken the safety precautions outlined in Part Eight.

4.   That you've done the negotiations outlined in Part Seven, and have adjusted the session to steer clear of any possible trouble areas. (For example, if being blindfolded is a limit for him, you can simply instruct him to keep his eyes closed.)

For several steps in this session, I'm suggesting both sexual and non-sexual alternatives to accommodate whatever play style you and your partner have negotiated. For the sexual play, I'm assuming the two of you are practicing safer sex; if you're in a long-term monogamous relationship, you can adjust the session accordingly. (I've indicated the places in the session where you should consider using barrier protection – condoms, Saran Wrap, dental dams or latex gloves.)

OK, here we go.

Step 1: Set the scene.

☐   Make sure the room is very warm. Dim the lights
        so that they're romantically soft, but still bright
        enough to see by.

☐   Dress in something that makes you feel powerful
        and sexy.

☐   Put on appropriate music (I like dramatic classical
        music, but let your own taste be your guide).

☐   Make sure you have easy access to the safety gear
        outlined in Part Eight.

Step 2. Prepare your equipment. Place the following toys
        on a nearby table, chair or nightstand:

☐   Collar

☐   Cock ring
        (alternative: soft leather thong or nylon cord, 4 to
        6 feet long)

☐   Paddle or slapper
        (alternative: flat-backed hairbrush or wooden
        kitchen spoon)

☐   Small multi-thonged whip
        (alternative: four 48" leather thongs, folded in half
        and rubber-banded together about an inch from
        the fold)

☐ Restraints
(alternative: never mind, just use rope)

☐ Four six-foot
lengths of rope

rope

☐ Four to six wooden
spring clothespins

☐ Blindfold
(alternative: scarf or large handkerchief)

☐ Condoms

☐ Lubricant

☐ Latex gloves

Step 3: Get in role.

☐ Sit on the bed or chair. Have him kneel at your
feet, in the following posture: knees apart about
12", hands on thighs, eyes lowered.

☐ Pick up his collar. Instruct him that once you've
put it on him, he is your slave and is to address
you as "Mistress." Ask him, "Do you want to serve
me as my slave?" When he says "Yes,"hold the
collar to his lips to be kissed. Tip his chin upward
with your hand. Look deeply into his eyes as you
fasten the collar around his neck. (If he does not
reply "yes," stop the session and renegotiate.)

☐ Have him stand in front of you, feet apart about 12", eyes lowered, hands down by his thighs. Fasten the cock ring (or tie the thong) firmly, but not painfully, around his cock and balls.

☐ Fasten a length of rope to his collar to use as a leash. Teach him to "heel," as follows: He is to walk a pace behind you, on your right (left if you're left-handed). When you stop walking, he is to revert to the standing posture you taught him earlier. If you snap your fingers, he is to kneel as you taught him. With the leash in your left hand and your light multi-thonged whip in your right, take him for a "walk" around the house, correcting him for mistakes with a light flick of the whip on his upper back or buttocks.

☐ End your walk at the bed. Sit down on the side of the bed and have him stand in front of you. Remove the leash. Attach the restraints to his wrists and ankles (or, if you're using rope, wrap a piece three or four times around each limb, leaving ends about two feet long) – but don't fasten them together yet.

Step 4: Teach him to serve you.

☐ Fasten a clothespin to each nipple. If he tolerates them well, tell him that they'll stay on until you're satisfied with his performance. (If he's obviously having a hard time with them, tell him you want him to keep them on for one minute, caress him and help him with the sensation until the time is up, then remove them.)

☐ If you've decided to play sexually, teach him how you like to have cunnilingus performed on you. (You may wish to use Saran Wrap or a dental dam as a safer-sex barrier.) As he eats you, direct him to the place, speed and technique you enjoy. If you want to have an orgasm or two, now is the time to do it (but don't get so carried away that you lose control of the session). Make mental notes of his mistakes, especially those he repeats after being cautioned.

☐ If you've decided not to play sexually, teach him to rub your feet. Use the same strategy outlined in the step above.

☐ When you've had enough, instruct him to stop. Gently remove the nipple clamps (remember, this is an especially strong sensation for him).

☐ Tell him how well he did overall. Then point out some of his mistakes to him. Tell him you're going to help him remember how to serve you better next time.

☐ Fasten his hands behind his back. Bend him over the edge of the bed. Spank him, starting gently with your hand, then building to fairly hard hand-spanks. Vary the speed and strength of the blows to see how he reacts. Try some smacks with the slapper (or hairbrush), building gradually and staying in touch with his reactions. As you spank, recount some of his mistakes to him and ask him if he's going to do better next time.

Step 5: Give him more sensations.

☐ If your bed has a headboard you can tie him to, unfasten his wrists; otherwise, leave them fastened behind his back. Have him lie on his back on the bed. If his wrists are behind him, place one or more pillows under his butt so there isn't too much pressure on them. If his wrists are free, tie them to the headboard.

☐ Tie his legs together at the ankles, using the restraints if he's wearing them. If there's a footboard you can use, tie his feet to it.

☐ Blindfold him.

☐ If you've agreed to play sexually, begin to masturbate his well-lubricated cock (using a glove or condom if necessary). If you think you might like to use your mouth on him, try to choose a lubricant that doesn't taste too yucky. Alternate masturbation with the types of sensation outlined below.

☐ Try the following sensations on his cock and balls:

– Slap his cock with the flat of your hand

– Bite it, building pressure gradually – not hard enough to break skin

– Scratch it – not hard enough to break skin, please

– Wrap your hand around the top of his scrotum and squeeze, building pressure gradually

– Whip his cock lightly (gather your multi-thonged whip into your hand so that the ends protrude by about 6", then flick the ends back and forth over the surface)

– Place clothespins on the loose skin of his scrotum, on the line of skin between his scrotum and asshole, or perhaps on the skin of his cock

☐ As you work on his genitals, pause occasionally to give sensations, ranging from gentle to moderately

strong, to the rest of his body. Pinch his nipples
(they should be OK by now), scratch his ribcage,
pinch his thighs, caress his chest and face.

☐   If you haven't agreed to play sexually, begin
thinking about how you're going to end your
session. Tell him you want him to accept a dozen
more whipstrokes to his cock and thighs, and then
you're going to untie him. Give him the strokes
hard enough that he'll have a little trouble
accepting them.

☐   Remove any clamps you have on him. Remember,
this will probably be a strong sensation for him.
Give him time to catch his breath after each clamp
comes off.

☐   If you have agreed to play sexually, either bring
him off with your hand or mouth or, if you like,
hop aboard and fuck him until he reaches orgasm.

Step 6: Winding down.

     Remove the blindfold and untie him. Hold him as
he comes back down to earth.

☐   Remove his collar and cock ring with the same
ceremony you used to put them on. Once they're
off, you're both out of role, back to your day-to-
day selves.

☐ Have a snack and a beverage together. While you eat, talk about the session – what worked, what didn't, what you'd like to do differently next time.

☐ The next day, contact him to see how he's doing. If either of you is experiencing any emotional aftereffects, schedule some time for a long, private face-to-face or telephone conversation in which you can discuss what's going on and make sure you both feel OK about it.

So that was it – your first dominant session. Congratulations!

If the session went well, you and your partner will probably both feel that you could go a little further next time. It's better to err on the side of caution, at least until you've played a few times.

Remember, this session is only "training wheels" until you develop your own bag of dominant tricks. Pay close attention to what feels comfortable and what doesn't, what turns you on and what doesn't, what works for him and what doesn't. As you learn more about your own domination style, you'll become more skillful and flexible.

12

Some notes for your submissive

Many women discover that they can deeply enjoy dominating their partners – if they're introduced to sexual domination in an understanding, appreciative and non-pushy way.

If you have submissive fantasies or experiences, and your lady is inexperienced but open-minded enough to consider exploring alternative sexual styles, here are some guidelines that will greatly increase your chances of success.

1. Don't "surprise" her. Although some people find this hard to understand, sexual domination is difficult and scary for many women. Your lady has spent her entire life being conditioned to be pleasant, accommodating and giving. She may be a little afraid of what your reaction will "really" be to her change in personality during your scene. Talk to her about your ideas at least

a week in advance; give her plenty of time to think about it, and plenty of reassurance as she does. If she doesn't feel comfortable with this style of play at this time, accept her "no" gracefully and lovingly. She may eventually come around to an interest in sexual domination, but she certainly won't if you nag her about it.

2. Be clear about who's giving what to whom. You may feel an impulse to "give" her your submission as a present. Reader, I have played both the dominant and submissive roles many times. Be completely clear about this: Her domination is her gift to you. Taking power, control and responsibility for the duration of a scene requires a tremendous outpouring of energy. If you want her to go on giving you the gift of sexual domination, be appreciative. (So what will you give her in return? Read on and I'll tell you.)

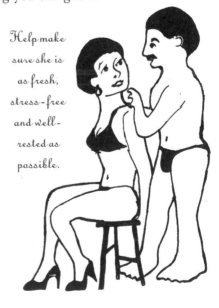

Help make sure she is as fresh, stress-free and well-rested as possible.

3. Help make sure she is as fresh, stress-free and well-rested as possible. A domination scene, especially a first domination scene,

requires a lot of energy. How about giving her a "day off" to prepare beforehand? Send the kids to your mother's, or take them out to lunch and the movies. Or, if you can afford it, give her a day of total pampering – facial, massage, manicure and pedicure, hairstyling, and so on – at your local full-service salon or spa. She'll be far more able to give you her best energy if she has some energy to spare!

4. Negotiate fully and honestly. Experienced dominants will not play with a partner who is less than honest about his needs and preferences. (One of the "three great lies" of S/M is "I'll do anything you want, Mistress.") Set aside at least an hour of uninterrupted time well before your session in which to discuss what activities might work well for both of you. A good structure to use is a three-part division: One category is for activities that both of you would find erotically exciting; one is for activities that one of you isn't excited by, but can accept if the other wants to try them; and the third is for activities that are a turnoff to either of you. If you've fantasized a lot about a particular activity, but not actually experienced it, be honest about that too – being hit with a riding crop can feel quite different in reality than it does in fantasy, and she needs to know that you may not like it as much as you thought you would.

5. Use safe words and "check-ins." A "safeword" – a code word that either of you can use to mean "this really isn't working for me; let's talk" – is an important reassurance for both the submissive and the dominant. If you've agreed on a safeword, you know that you can beg, cry or whatever turns you on, and she knows that whatever she's doing is still basically OK with you. Also, arrange for her to "check in" with you every so often during the scene. She can quietly ask you, "How are you doing?" or "Still with me?" A soft "I'm OK, mistress," or even a "thumbs up" signal, lets her know that the scene is still working for you.

6. Be realistic in your expectations. Please, please don't expect this first scene to be the hottest, wildest scene you've ever dreamed about or experienced. (You don't drive the Indianapolis 500 the day after you get your driver's license.) If your scene ends up with both of you having had a nice time, and feeling loving and intimate with one another, that's a good beginning.

7. Give her plenty of positive strokes. Remember, she's given you a great gift. A day or so after your scene, sit down to discuss how it went. If something happened that didn't work for you, be honest about it, but for heaven's sake don't be harsh or critical – she was doing her best. Tell her about the things that did work for you and how excited they made you feel. And make

sure she knows how grateful you are for the energy she gave and the emotional risk she took for you.

I know, I know – you've been fantasizing for months, if not years, and it's tough to be gentle and supportive when you're aching to submit your body and soul to her. But I feel sure that if more submissive men follow guidelines like these when they introduce their partners to erotic power play, there will soon be a lot more dominant women in the world. And won't that be a great thing for all of us?

13

Tips on partner-finding

I get a lot of letters asking for help and guidance from people who are struggling to find compatible partners for female-dominant play – either casual or lifetime.

I thought I'd spend this chapter sharing with you the strategies and attitudes that have worked for many of the people I know. These ideas will work, for the most part, for men or women and for dominants or submissives. Men and submissives may have to work harder and be more patient before finding the play partners they seek – but I think that, with time, creativity and savvy, anybody can find compatible, sane, pleasant potential partners. Here are some ideas to start you off:

– *Tip 1. Be clear on what you're looking for.* If what you want is to give a good spanking, a partner whose primary kink is domestic service is probably not going to be a good fit for you. If you want a spouse, you probably don't want to spend your time playing with someone already in a committed relationship. Get clear in your own mind about your needs, desires, and limits, and practice talking about them until you can explain them comfortably to someone else.

If you're submissive, you may feel that your only desire is to fulfill someone else's desires. That sounds exciting, but it's not really very useful information – it's kind of like being asked, "What do you want for dinner?" and responding "Food." Virtually all submissives get off on knowing that they're fulfilling their partner's desires – that's what makes them submissives. Still, I assure you that if your partner's desires aren't a reasonably good match for yours, you'll find yourself frustrated, horny and burned out in a very short time. If you're not too sure what your own needs are, here's a good question to ponder: How will you know when you've fulfilled your mistress's desires? Will you have experienced pain? Will you have accomplished a task? Will you have given her an orgasm?

– *Tip 2. Be flexible.* This sounds a bit like a contradiction with Tip 1, but it isn't, really. Anybody you connect with is going to have needs and desires of his or her own, and not all of them will correspond exactly with yours. If you're too specific in demanding exactly what you want, without giving your partner a chance to be creative and to seek out his or her own rewards, you'll lose a play partner.

A good exercise would be to distinguish between your "wants" and your "needs." What do you absolutely need from your play in order to consider it worthwhile? Bondage? Pain? Sex? Service? A fetish? If there are more than one or two items on your "needs" list, consider whether you need to expand your repertoire a bit. Try fantasizing about something outside your old tried-and-true favorites, and see if you can discover some new avenues for exploration.

Tip 3. Let go of some expectations. Very few mistresses look like the blond goddesses in the glossy magazines. (In fact, I've met quite a few of the women who advertise in such magazines, and *they* mostly don't look like that.) Very few slaves are young, gorgeous, service-oriented and earning six figures a year. You are not going to find a partner like one of those – I promise.

Somewhere out there is a dominant or a submissive who's perfect for you in many ways.

S/he's kinky, creative, loving, sane and fun to be with. Do you really care if s/he's a few years older or a few pounds heavier or a few bucks poorer than the creature of your fantasies?

— *Tip 4. Consider improving your own packaging.* Nobody wants you to starve yourself or spend all your time primping just to find a partner. However, now is a good time to take a quick personal inventory to see if there are any areas where a little sprucing up might be required.

On the physical side, a partner who is reasonably fit, and who has the energetic and optimistic outlook which exercise brings, is going to be more sought-after than his or her couch potato counterpart. Also, neatness counts – if you're not already in the habit of being clean and neat, with teeth and clothing in good repair, now is the time to start.

On the emotional side, please do yourself and your future partner a favor by making sure you're not bringing any major emotional baggage into the relationship. Sexual domination is not a substitute for therapy – if you have stuff that needs to be talked about, find yourself a competent professional and get talking. In particular, I've seen more promising relationships founder on the rocks of substance abuse than any other problem: if you're wondering if perhaps you're drinking or drugging a teeny bit too much, solve that problem – with the help of an appropriate support group if necessary – before you go hunting.

Also, sexual domination is not an appropriate venue in which to act out genuine dislike. If you don't like men, or women, or redheads, or whatever, the best thing for you *and* them is to work out your problems in therapy and leave them alone. Play sexual domination games only with people you like and care about.

Tip 5. Learn to make conversation. Many players' pet peeve is being cruised by potential partners who can't or won't talk about anything but sex or dominance. While there's certainly a time and a place for a direct request, asking someone you've just met whether she likes anal play is likely to be a turn-off. Instead, learn to ask good questions and to listen to the answers – everybody enjoys being listened to by an attentive and attractive partner.

If your conversational skills are weak, many local organizations teach classes in flirting, assertiveness, conversational skills and so on. Such a class would almost certainly be a good investment of your partner-finding time and money.

–   *Tip 6. What do you have to offer?* Are you smart? Funny? For bottoms, do you give a great footrub and enjoy doing it? Can you fix a car or hang a window? Do you process pain well? Do you know all the best nightspots and love a night on the town dancing? For tops, are you a whiz with a flogger? Do you have a stern expression? Do you have a gift for role-playing? All of these are assets that can help attract a partner to you. Sit down with a piece of paper sometime and write down everything you're good at and enjoy doing. Be sure and pat yourself on the back a lot while you write, because self-confidence is the most attractive quality of all.

–   *Tip 7. Get on the Internet.* For kinky people in this day and age, not being on the 'Net is like not knowing how to read. The Internet offers information, products, personal ads, the chance to "chat" on-line with like-minded folks, a way to learn new techniques and new ways to make your play safer and hotter, and a lot more.

Yes, you will encounter a lot of jerks and know-nothings and clueless commercial types, and, yes, getting there requires a certain commitment of time and money (not as much of either as you might expect). It's still worth it.

If you're not sure where to start, some resources are listed in the appendix.

– *Tip 8. Be a joiner.* Even if you've never joined a club or support group in your life, make an exception for your local BDSM club. Most clubs offer regular meetings where you can meet people with interests similar to yours – and people with different interests, which can be even more fun. The more actively you participate, the more likely you'll be to become well known and to meet potential friends, mentors and partners.

If you don't live in an area that has a BDSM club, consider starting one – *SM 101* has a whole chapter on forming BDSM communities. One way to find out if there's enough interest near you is to put together a "munch" – a get-together of kinkyfolk in a restaurant or bar, just for chat and friendship. Munches are usually promoted on the Internet.

– *Tip 9. Don't overlook personal ads.* I know an increasing number of couples who have met through personals – either on-line or in their local lifestyle paper. A good personal ad should be clear about what you have to offer and what you're looking for, and intriguing enough to catch people's attention. It's OK to put in some of your "not-so-good" stuff – if the fact that you smoke, or are overweight, or whatever, is a deal-breaker for someone, it's better not to waste their time or yours. Ideally, you should get only a few responses, and they should be very close to what you're seeking. If you get a lot of responses, you've written too general an ad.

– *Tip 10. Make kinky friends.* I've seen people who are seeking partners attend events, or hang out in kinky environments, and utterly ignore anybody who isn't of the gender or orientation that interests them. This is a big mistake.

You can learn a lot from people who aren't potential partners for you. They can give you feedback about how to improve your desirability as a top or a bottom, they can introduce you to other people, they can "mentor" you into private discussion groups and party environments, and a lot more.

It pays in kink environments to be as outgoing and friendly as possible toward people of all backgrounds. If you can't find a lover right now, a friend is at least as good... and, with luck, patience and skill, the lover(s) will follow.

appendix

How to go further

If you've read all the information in this book carefully, you've just graduated from kindergarten as a sexually dominant woman.

If you want to go on to grade school, high school, even college (!), you'll need a lot more information than I can give you here. Some of it you'll have to discover on your own. But there are several good books, periodicals and clubs that can help improve your skills and techniques.

My partner Jay Wiseman's *SM 101: A Realistic Introduction* is an excellent overview of fundamentals. Other great how-to books include Race Bannon's *Learning the Ropes*, Pat Califia's *Sensuous Magic*, John Warren's *The Loving Dominant*, and Miller and Devon's *Screw the Roses, Send Me the Thorns*. *Different Loving*, by Brame, Brame and Jacobs, is an excellent collection of information and interviews about various playstyles and people in the fetish, S/M and related scenes. All should be available at erotic boutiques, leather stores, gay, lesbian and many mainstream bookstores, and from on-line vendors.

I've also co-authored two books under a different pen name: *The Bottoming Book: Or, How to Get Terrible Things Done to You By Wonderful People*, and *The Topping Book: Or, Getting Good at Being Bad*. Both are designed to help you and your partner deal with some of the physical, emotional and spiritual ramifications of this form of play.

To improve your knot-tying skills, consider picking up a copy of the *Boy Scout Handbook* or *The Klutz Book of Knots*. If you enjoy spanking, try my *The Compleat Spanker*. If you'd like to get better at role-playing, you may find helpful ideas in Carol Queen's *Exhibitionism for the Shy*.

Some of the more realistic scene magazines include *Prometheus* (the publication of New York's The Eulenspiegel Society), *Sandmutopian Guardian*, *Boudoir Noir* and *Kinky People, Places and Things*.

If you're looking for a therapist, counselor, physician or other health care practitioner who will not be judgmental about your interest in sexual domination, the Kink-Aware Professionals list at http://www.bannon.com/~race/kap lists such people throughout the U.S. Also, San Francisco Sex Information at 415/787-SFSI offers referrals to sexuality resources in the Bay Area, and some nationwide resources.

The Internet provides a wealth of information about sexual domination and related practices. In Usenet, try the newsgroups soc.subculture.bondage-bdsm, soc.subculture.bondage-bdsm.femdom and soc.sexuality.spanking. On the World Wide Web, do a search on "BDSM." On AOL, do a keyword search on "passion@thrive." Or go to bdsm.miningco.com for great information and links to other resources. And of course, you can always check out the Greenery Press website at www.bigrock.com/~greenery. (Internet resources change rapidly, so if any of these resources have gone out of date by the time you read this book, you may have to do some searching to find more current resources.)

A word of warning on the Internet: Anyone can post there. Use your common sense. In particular, if information you read there seems unrealistic, dangerous, or based on philosophies that make you uncomfortable, steer clear. Much of the "information" on the Internet is designed as masturbation material, not clear guidelines for safe and responsible play. Enjoy the pictures and stories if you like, but don't imitate them unless you feel certain that the behavior portrayed there is safe and within you and your partner's limits. A big hint: very little good information appears on the sites that cost money to access.

Many kinky folks use the Internet to set up get-togethers called "munches," which are social events held in restaurants. These are a great, non-threatening way to meet friendly people and learn more about the art and craft of female domination. If there aren't any munches in your area, you can start one yourself.

Many cities now have BDSM-oriented nightclubs – often a regular dance club which has designated a certain night of the week as "fetish night" or some such. In general, I don't think much of these: they're usually not well supervised, and alcohol and sexual domination are a very poor combination.

Instead of the nightclubs, consider joining your local support group. Most major metropolitan areas have one or more BDSM clubs. Some of the largest include the Society of Janus here in the Bay Area (www.soj.org) and the Eulenspiegel Society in New York (www.tes.org). Other cities have clubs of their own. If you live within driving distance of a city, I strongly recommend that you join such a club – it's a good way to meet other people who play with sexual domination, and many clubs publish newsletters full of events and information. Even if you don't live near a city, join one of the major clubs so you can read the newsletter and hear about the events. Several World Wide Web sites (including those of the clubs above) run extensive listings of local clubs and support groups, as do most of the magazines I've listed here.

If you get involved in your local organization, you may at some point find yourself thinking about attending a "play party" – an event where people get together to play, watch or simply socialize. At such parties, you are usually welcome to stay in the social area and enjoy the food and company, to sit quietly and unobtrusively in the play area and watch the scenes going on, or to play. At most parties, there is usually at least one Dungeon Monitor on duty at all times, to make sure the party rules are being obeyed as well as to answer questions and to help out by bringing water, safer sex supplies, and so on. Parties can be a fun way to indulge your exhibitionistic (or voyeuristic) side and to meet new folks.

If you're looking for information or a resource that I haven't mentioned here, feel free to write or e-mail me and I'll do my best to answer your questions. My address is:

Lady Green
3739 Balboa Ave. #195
San Francisco, CA 94121
http://www.bigrock.com/~greenery

GENERAL SEXUALITY

DIY Porn Handbook: A How-To Guide to Documenting Our Own Sexual Revolution
Madison Young $56.95

The Explorer's Guide to Planet Orgasm: for every body *(Spring 2017)*
Annie Sprinkle $13.95

A Hand in the Bush: The Fine Art of Vaginal Fisting
Deborah Addington $13.95

The Jealousy Workbook: Exercises and Insights for Managing Open Relationships
Kathy Labriola $19.95

Love In Abundance: A Counselor's Advice on Open Relationships
Kathy Labriola $15.95

Miss Vera's Cross-Gender Fun for All
Veronica Vera $14.95

Phone Sex: Oral Skills and Aural Thrills
Miranda Austin $15.95

Tricks... To Please a Man
Tricks... To Please a Woman
Jay Wiseman . . . . $13.95 ea.

When Someone You Love Is Kinky
Dossie Easton & Catherine A. Liszt . . . $15.95

BDSM/KINK

The Artisan's Book of Fetishcraft: Patterns and Instructions for Creating Professional Fetishwear, Restraints & Equipment
John Huxley $27.95

Conquer Me: girl-to-girl wisdom about fulfilling your submissive desires
Kacie Cunningham $13.95

Miss Vera's Cross Gender Fun for All
Dr. Veronica Vera $14.95

Family Jewels: A Guide to Male Genital Play and Torment
Hardy Haberman $12.95

Flogging
Joseph Bean $11.95

The Human Pony: A Guide for Owners, Trainers and Admirers
Rebecca Wilcox $27.95

Intimate Invasions: The Ins and Outs of Erotic Enema Play
M.R. Strict $13.95

The Mistress Manual: a good girl's guide to female dominance
Mistress Lorelei Powers $16.95

The (New and Improved) Loving Dominant
John Warren $16.95

The New Bottoming Book
The New Topping Book
Dossie Easton & Janet W. Hardy . . . $14.95 ea.

Playing Well With Others: Your Field Guide to Discovering, Exploring and Navigating the Kink, Leather and BDSM Communities
Lee Harrington & Mollena Williams . . . $19.95

Play Piercing
Deborah Addington $13.95

Radical Ecstasy: SM Journeys to Transcendence
Dossie Easton & Janet W. Hardy $16.95

The Seductive Art of Japanese Bondage
Midori, photographs by Craig Morey . . $27.95

SM 101: A Realistic Introduction
Jay Wiseman $24.95

Spanking for Lovers
Janet W. Hardy $15.95

TOYBAG GUIDES:
A Workshop In A Book $9.95 each

Age Play, by Lee "Bridgett" Harrington

Basic Rope Bondage, by Jay Wiseman

Chastity Play, by Miss Simone

Clips and Clamps, by Jack Rinella

Dungeon Emergencies & Supplies, by Jay Wiseman

Hot Wax and Temperature Play, by Spectrum

Playing With Taboo, by Mollena Williams

Greenery Press books are available from your favorite on-line or brick-and-mortar bookstore or erotic boutique. If you are having trouble locating the book you want, please contact us at 541-683-0961. These and other Greenery Press books are also available in ebook format from all major ebook retailers.